Gavin Kilduff

fr. CNS
Election Day
nov. 8/55

H.F. Hosp.
B'klyn

SAINTS

FROM THE

NATIONAL GALLERY

SAINT GEORGE

from a predella by Crivelli (No. 724)

A FEW SAINTS

FROM PICTURES IN THE

NATIONAL GALLERY

With Notes by

MARTIN DAVIES

1946

PRINTED FOR THE TRUSTEES

LONDON

Q
755
L 847

PRINTED IN ENGLAND
BY HARRISON AND SONS LTD.
PRINTERS TO HIS MAJESTY THE KING
44—47 ST. MARTIN'S LANE, LONDON, W.C.2

Most of the photographs have been taken specially by
Mrs. Wilson and Mrs. Tierney.

SAINT ALBERT THE GREAT

Albertus Magnus was not officially beatified when
the original of the accompanying plate was painted ;
but the Dominicans—and Fra Angelico was a
Dominican—have always and rightly been proud
of him. Albert was greatly distinguished for his
learning and is often referred to as the *Universal
Doctor ;* he has been partly overshadowed by the
fame of his pupil Aquinas, who merited the still
grander title of *Angelic Doctor.*

When Albertus Magnus was in Paris, no building
could contain the students wishing to hear him. He
therefore lectured in the open ; the spot was called
the *Place de Maître Albert,* now the Place Maubert.

PLATE I : *from a predella by the*
Blessed Angelico (No. 663)

SAINT ANTHONY
THE GREAT

One day a bowman came across S. Anthony and his monks at play. He uttered words of blame, to which S. Anthony replied, " Shoot ! " ; and the bowman shot. " Shoot again—and again " ; but after three times the bowman said he must not keep his bow always taut. " Even so," S. Anthony triumphantly answered, " the servants of God must sometimes relax."

It is sad that this lesson of moderation was not a subject illustrated by the old painters ; on the contrary, S. Anthony in pictures is notorious for disgusting violence. The story of the bowman, nevertheless, does exist ; for which reason incidents typical of monasticism have been reserved for another and indeed a suitable man, S. Benedict.

* A rather similar story is related of S. John the Evangelist.

PLATE II: *from an altarpiece ascribed to Orcagna, Jacopo di Cione and Assistants (No. 569)*

SAINT BENEDICT (1)

S. Benedict when still young retired from
Rome to a cave at Subiaco. There he was
assailed by the thought of a beautiful
woman he had seen in Rome; but he
conquered temptation by rolling naked in
the brambles outside his cave. The
brambles are now roses; opinion is divided
whether they became so at once, or when
S. Francis blessed them several centuries
later.

Margaritone in this plate has shown
S. Benedict without any doubt; but what
is the other figure? Can it be Temptation,
warming its hands (one might imagine) at
hell fire?

PLATE III : *from a picture by Margaritone* (No. 564)

SAINT BENEDICT (2)

S. Placidus once went out to get water and fell into the river. S. Benedict learnt of the danger by revelation and sent S. Maurus to help, who walked over the water as if it had been land, seized S. Placidus by the hair and saved his life. S. Benedict attributed the miracle to the Holy Obedience of S. Placidus.

The Benedictine habit is properly black; but certain reformed Benedictines wore white. One of these communities was the Camaldolese, for whom the picture illustrated was doubtless made; the painter, Lorenzo Monaco, was himself a Camaldolese monk.

PLATE IV : *from a predella by Lorenzo Monaco (No.* 4062)

SAINT BERNARD

S. Bernard the Cistercian is distinguished in the arts. The Cistercians wanted churches solidly built and nothing more; they renounced the gaudiness of Romanesque decoration, and could almost be said to have invented Gothic architecture. What Gothic eventually became in the cathedral of Beauvais was, of course, far from their intention; but their work is most important in the history of the nascent style, and some Cistercian forms, especially in Italy, were in general use for centuries. How far S. Bernard himself was concerned in practical building is doubtful; he was frequently rapt in visions, once travelling for a whole day by the Lake of Geneva without noticing that there *was* a lake. But he inveighed against Romanesque sculpture, perhaps that of Vézelay which he probably knew; and his spirit seems indeed allied to Cistercian Gothic —did not Walter Pater write of "those lightsome aisles of Pontigny, so expressive of the purity, the lowly sweetness, of the soul of Bernard"?

In poetry as well as in architecture, S. Bernard has a place of the first rank. When Dante has ascended through Paradise to the Empyrean, his own Beatrice leaves him; her place is taken by S. Bernard, whose prayer to the Virgin for Dante's final revelation is celebrated.

Dante thus imagines the great mystic:

> *Diffuso era per li occhi e per le gene*
> *di benigna letizia, in atto pio*
> *quale a tenero padre si convene.**

Filippo Lippi's conception differs, but is defensible also.

---

* His features shone with tender joy; holy his attitude, fatherly his kindness.

PLATE V : *from a picture by Filippo Lippi (No. 248)*

SAINT CATHERINE
OF ALEXANDRIA

S. Catherine of Alexandria is a principal
Patroness of learning. She appears with
great frequency in old pictures, either in
mystic union with the Infant Christ or
holding a wheel, instrument of her
tortures. The wheel did not kill her ;
she was beheaded, and angels carried her
body to the summit of Mount Sinai, as
Margaritone limpidly shows. A more
elegant representation of S. Catherine is
illustrated under the heading *Martyrs*.

PLATE VI : *from a picture by Margaritone (No. 564)*

SAINT CATHERINE OF SIENA

S. Catherine of Siena is a phenomenon of the
XIV century; by spiritual authority alone she
became a powerful force in Italy, and frequently
wrote letters to the Pope telling him what to do.
She is here shown before her canonization, and so
without a halo, and is correctly dressed as a
Dominican Tertiary with a *white* head-covering.
She is frequently and improperly represented with
the Stigmata, or Impressions of the Five Wounds of
Christ, but not here. Two other Dominican
worthies in other parts of this picture are justifiably
shown with the Stigmata ; S. Margaret of Hungary
and the Blessed Walter of Strasbourg.

PLATE VII : *from a predella by the Blessed*
Angelico (No. 663)

SAINT CHRISTOPHER

S. Christopher was a giant and it came into his mind to serve the greatest king in the world. He thought that he had found the right man, until a minstrel sang a song about the Devil; the king crossed himself each time the Devil was named, and confessed he did it as a defence against the Devil's power. Clearly the Devil was stronger than the king. S. Christopher went in search of the Devil and found him and served him, until he shied at a wayside Crucifix. It appeared that Christ was strongest of all, and S. Christopher set out in search of Christ. After a time he found a hermit, who said : " To serve Christ, you must often fast." " I will not." " You must often pray." " I will not." " There is a dangerous river nearby ; if you carry travellers across the stream, it would be pleasing to Christ." S. Christopher agreed to that ; he built himself a hut by the river and cut himself a stick for support in the water and carried travellers across. After a time a Child asked to be taken. S. Christopher put the Child on his shoulder and entered the stream ; but the water rose and rose, and the Child became at each instant heavier, until S. Christopher was afraid. When they were across at last he said " Child, if I had had the whole world on my shoulders, it could not have been heavier " ; to which the Child replied, " You have indeed carried the whole world and its Creator too, for I am the Christ you are seeking ; as a sign of which, plant your stick in the ground, tomorrow it will be leafy." And the next day it was indeed like a palm-tree, with leaves and dates.

PLATE VIII: *from a picture by*
Moretto (No. 1025)

SAINT COSMAS AND SAINT DAMIAN

SS. Cosmas and Damian were the doctors who never took fees ; they were very popular. They are Patrons of Florence, and Cosimo is the name of several members of the Medici family ; they appear therefore often in Florentine pictures, and should be dressed alike, as here.

Several odd stories about them perhaps indicate respect for the triumphs of medicine. A man whose leg was eaten away by a canker slept ; SS. Cosmas and Damian with knives and unguents appeared. S. Cosmas : " Where shall we get good flesh to replace the rotten flesh, when we have cut it away ? " S. Damian : " An Ethiopian was buried only today in the cemetery nearby," and he went and cut off the Ethiopian's leg and brought it. Then SS. Cosmas and Damian cut off the sick man's leg and fastened on the other instead. When the man awoke, he felt no pain ; he lit a candle and " thought he had become someone else " ; when he had collected his senses, he " fell out of bed for joy." The people went to the Ethiopian's tomb and found the body with a leg missing, and a white leg lying near. This story is sometimes illustrated.

PLATE IX : *from a predella by the Blessed Angelico (No. 663)*

SAINT DOMINIC

This lovely picture has been sometimes wrongly
considered. It is not by Gentile Bellini ; it bears a
genuine signature of Giovanni Bellini. It is not a
portrait of Fra Teodoro da Urbino, to which the
emblems of S. Dominic have been added ; it was
always a S. Dominic. It is indeed possible that
this Fra Teodoro sat to Bellini as a *model* ; which
might explain why the character is not quite
satisfactory. The saint is there,

> *l'amoroso drudo*
> *della fede cristiana ;*

the fighter is perhaps not there,

> *il santo atleta*
> *benigno a' suoi, ed a'nemici crudo.**

* The amorous swain of the faith of Christ ; the
athlete saint, kind to his friends and cruel to his enemies.

PLATE X : *a picture by Giovanni Bellini (No.* 1440)

SAINT DOROTHY

When S. Dorothy was tortured on account of her faith, she suffered everything patiently for the love of Jesus Christ, in whose garden (she said) she had gathered delightful roses and apples. As she was being led off to be beheaded, one Theophilus asked her scornfully to let him have some of those roses. The season was winter; but when S. Dorothy knelt down on the block, a Child appeared brilliantly clad, carrying a basket with three roses and three apples. Take them, the Virgin Martyr begged, to Theophilus; the Child, who was Christ Himself, did so, and Theophilus was converted and received forthwith the crown of martyrdom.

PLATE XI : *a picture by Francesco di Giorgio (No.* 1682)

SAINT EDWARD THE CONFESSOR

Saint Edward the Confessor was for a time the Patron of England, but has been supplanted by S. George; he was a principal benefactor of Westminster Abbey.

The ring he holds in the illustration refers to the following story. S. Edward was passing through a village, where the church was being consecrated in the name of S. John the Evangelist. The king stopped for the ceremony, and a fair old man begged alms; S. Edward had nothing to give except a ring he wore. Later, two English pilgrims had lost their way in the Holy Land; but the old man appeared to them to comfort them, and said, " I am John the Evangelist; give back this ring to your king who gave it to me, and tell him that in half a year he shall rejoice in Heaven with me." Thereupon the pilgrims fell asleep; and when they awoke, they were not in Palestine, but there were flocks of sheep, and shepherds who answered their questions in English, and it was in Kent on Barham Down. The pilgrims hastened to the king and gave him the ring; and six months after, S. Edward died.

PLATE XII : *from The Wilton Diptych (No. 4451)*

SAINT ELOY

The illustration does not represent S. Eloy himself but the Cross is likely to have been his work. He was a goldsmith ; the Cross is copied, and no doubt fairly exactly, from a Cross formerly in the Abbey of Saint-Denis near Paris and ascribed in several old inventories to S. Eloy.

S. Eloy was also, it is said, a blacksmith. He had some difficulty in shoeing restive horses, or perhaps it was one particularly *devilish* horse ; but a young man, who may have been Christ, successfully helped him. The horse was tied up apart ; the leg was detached for S. Eloy to shoe comfortably; and when the operation was completed, the leg was put back on the horse. This scene is illustrated not infrequently ; there are also single figures of S. Eloy holding a detached hoof, which is indeed his proper attribute.

PLATE XIII : *from a picture by the Master of S. Giles (No. 4681)*

SAINT ERASMUS

The theory of what has happened to S. Erasmus in art is due to the ingenious Father Cahier. S. Erasmus was a nautical saint, perhaps because an angel wafted him over the sea to Formia in Italy; in any case, he was a favourite with Mediterranean sailors, and *S. Elmo's fire** is a phrase still used for the electrical lights that appear sometimes in the rigging of ships. A capstan with a bit of rope round it is therefore supposed to have been his attribute. Such a thing sculptured or painted in places far from the sea meant nothing, and people were used to seeing saints with the instruments of their martyrdom; it was an easy deduction that his intestines were wound out of him by a windlass. The next step was to represent the martyrdom itself; even Poussin in the XVII Century painted the details !

Cahier's theory is that this story is invented; the torture is described in some late accounts of S. Erasmus, who is stated to have survived it.

* S. Elmo is surely S. Erasmus; but curiously enough the name is often misapplied to the Blessed Peter Gonzalez, a Dominican also represented in this picture.

PLATE XIV : *from a predella by the*
Blessed Angelico (No. 663)

SAINT FRANCIS (1)

His name was John. His father, who was a merchant, thought it useful that he should learn French; the urchins of Assisi used to laugh at him, "*Il Francesco ! Il Francesco !*" *Francesco* stuck, and a Christian name was thus invented.

The great miracle of the Franciscan Order was the Stigmatization of its founder on Mount Alvernia :—

> *Nel crudo sasso intra Tevere e Arno*
> *de Cristo prese l'ultimo sigillo,*
> *che le sue membra due anni portarno.**

In pictorial art the character of the scene was fixed by Giotto; Sassetta, although his merits are naturally different, has tried to preserve something of Giotto's grand tradition.

It would be improper here to comment on the miracle itself; but it is necessary to emphasize that most pictures, including the one illustrated, differ in important points from the best written accounts. It suffices to mention one; Brother Leo was *not* a witness to the event.

---

* There is a bare rock between Tiber and Arno; there from Christ he received the final seal, two years impressed upon his limbs. (The two previous seals were the approval of the Franciscan Order by successive Popes.)

PLATE XV : *a picture by Sassetta (No. 4760)*

SAINT FRANCIS (2)

This sombre penitent, with sagging mouth and up-cast eyes, hugging a skull, is also almost certainly S. Francis. What has happened to him ? S. Francis was indeed passionately ascetic and mystic ; but he loved his brother the Sun, and sombre he never was.

This image of XVII century Spain can be rectified by what S. Francis himself wrote about Death :

Laudatu si mi signore per sora nostra morte corporale
da la quale nullu homo vivente po skampare :
guai a quilli ke morrano in peccato mortale :
beati quilli ke se trovarà ne le tue sanctissime voluntati
*ka la morte secunda non li poterà far male.**

* Praise my Lord for sister Bodily Death, which no living man can escape ; woe to them that shall die in mortal sin ; blessed are they that shall be found within Thy most holy laws, for the death of the soul can never harm them.

PLATE XVI : *a picture by Zurbárán (No. 230)*

SAINT HELEN

This famous picture is iconographically a poor thing. S. Helen may have had some such vision, but it is quite pointless—she wanted to know where the True Cross was concealed. In any case, she was about eighty at the time. If, puzzled, one enquires further, one finds that the figure is cribbed from an engraving of the School of Marcantonio, which in its turn is from a Parmigiano drawing inscribed *Danae*. It is true that many early Christian churches are built of fragments of Pagan temples, and that Dante sometimes quotes Virgil with a complete change of meaning, but these things are justified by the taste in which they are done. I doubt if Veronese knew what he was about ; for a Christian saint in ecstasy ought not to be in such an attitude.

The iconographical faults may be due partly to a tradition of vagueness at Venice ; Vasari had tried in vain to understand the subjects of Giorgione's frescoes. But there exists proof of Veronese's personal muddleheadedness in his testimony before the Inquisition. The affair was on account of buffoons and German soldiers introduced into a religious picture, the *Feast in the House of Simon*. That subject is distinguished from other *Feasts* in the Gospel story by the presence of the Magdalen (or Mary of Bethany) anointing the feet of Christ ; Veronese had painted a dog instead of the Magdalen, and saw no reason to change it. Indeed, I believe that the only alteration effected by the Inquisitors was—the title ! For the picture, which is in the Academy at Venice, is now inscribed *Feast in the House of Levi*. The evidence is interesting ; Veronese defended his buffoons and German soldiers by the tradition of the Great Artists, and when asked what he meant, stated that in Michelangelo's *Last Judgment* the figures are shamefully naked. The Inquisitor retorted that at the Last Judgment everyone may well *be* naked, and in any case what had that to do with buffoons and German soldiers ?

PLATE XVII : *a picture by Veronese (No.* 1041)

SAINT HUBERT

A picture of a huntsman and a stag with a
Crucifix between its horns may be the
Vision of S. Eustace or of S. Hubert.
S. Eustace, or Placidus as he was then
called, was a Roman soldier; S. Hubert
was a courtier. They both were fond of
hunting and both were converted to
sanctity by a mysterious stag, which
reproved them. It is often very difficult
to tell them apart with certainty. In an
Italian picture the man is likely to be
S. Eustace, in a Netherlandish or German
picture he is likely to be S. Hubert; and
S. Eustace ought to be shown dressed as a
soldier.

PLATE XVIII : *a picture by the Master of Werden (No. 252)*

SAINT IGNATIUS

Not Loyola ; this S. Ignatius was a pillar
of the early Church. Throughout the
torments of his martyrdom he never
ceased to invoke the name of Jesus Christ ;
his torturers asked him why, and he replied,
That Name is written in my heart. When
he was dead, they took out his heart and
cut it open ; within it in golden letters was
the sacred Name. Angelico shows the
heart whole and not cut open ; but there
is no doubt that he has here represented
S. Ignatius.

PLATE XIX : *from a predella by the Blessed Angelico (No. 663)*

SAINT JEROME (1)

S. Jerome when a young man believed in Christ; but he read for pleasure Cicero, and the Eastern style of the Prophets repelled him. After a time he fell very ill. His life was despaired of; in a vision he was brought before the throne of God, Who asked him his religion. " Christian." " You lie; you are a Ciceronian," and God ordered him to be severely beaten. S. Jerome cried out for mercy, which was granted when he had signed a promise never to read any classical authors again. Thereupon he woke up in his bed, perfectly well except for his weals.

This story is told by S. Jerome himself.

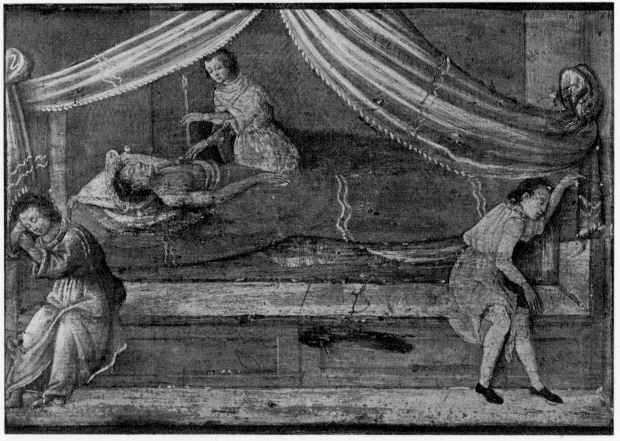

PLATE XX : *from a predella by Botticini (No. 227)*

SAINT JEROME (2)

A visitor to picture galleries soon learns that S. Jerome had
a lion. As a matter of history, the lion and his adventures
belong more properly to another Palestinian recluse of similar
name, S. Gerasimus; it was called *Jordan*, and died of grief
on the tomb of its master. S. Gerasimus nevertheless was not
a subject for the old painters; they thought they were
representing S. Jerome.

When S. Jerome had taken a thorn from the lion's paw,
it became tame and was given the office of guarding an ass
belonging to the monastery. One day, the lion slept; some
merchants with their camels were passing and stole the ass.
The lion returned shamefacedly to the Monastery, where the
monks thought it had eaten the ass; S. Jerome condemned it
to doing the ass's work of carrying wood and so on. Later,
the merchants and their camels and the ass passed that way
again. The lion recognized the ass with a roar that scattered
the merchants, and drove both ass and camels to the monastery;
the merchants followed as soon as they dared, and knelt to ask
pardon of S. Jerome.

PLATE XXI : *from a picture ascribed to Patenier (No. 4826)*

SAINT JOHN THE BAPTIST

Pictures of the Virgin, the Infant Christ and the Infant S. John the Baptist together are so frequent, and so often remembered as beautiful, that one does not naturally question the subject ; but there is no authority for it in the Bible. There exist some legends, as of the two Children meeting in the desert, which might seem at first to be possible sources for the theme, but almost certainly are not ; there is one passage in the *Meditations* ascribed to S. Bonaventura that could be the origin of it, but no one has been able to prove that it certainly is. The motive itself does not appear until the second half of the XV Century at Florence. It is probable that the Florentine artists' delight in *putti*, and the fact that S. John the Baptist was the city's Patron Saint greatly increased its popularity; but I rather doubt if any painter or sculptor at that time would have thought of it unaided. Such iconographical caprices—for so it would be, if popularity had not chanced to standardize it—were invented later on by individualists like Leonardo or Michelangelo, but probably not by the earlier men such as Filippo Lippi or even Donatello.

PLATE XXII: *an altarpiece by Leonardo da Vinci (No. 1093)*

SAINT JOHN
THE EVANGELIST

The picture shows S. John surrounded by several
incidents of the Apocalypse. The Son of Man
with a sickle in His hand is mentioned in Ch. XIV,
v. 14; the Woman and Child and the Dragon in
Ch. XII; and the four Angels in the four corners
of the world holding the four winds in Ch. VII,
v. 1. The winds are symbolized as lions, which
seems to be in a tradition peculiar to Florence,*
and perhaps appears first in a fresco by Giotto.
In any case, the whole picture is closely derived
from Giotto; Giovanni dal Ponte's only additions
are pen, paper and ink for S. John.

* Scenes from S. John's story similar to the Florentine
traditions, and in particular with the winds as beasts
occur later on in Spain.

PLATE XXIII: *from a predella by Giovanni dal Ponte (No. 580)*

SAINT JOHN GUALBERTO

S. John Gualberto, like so many, was not born a
Saint. He was a Florentine; his brother was
murdered—he knew who had done it and plotted
vengeance, but could not find his opportunity. And
then one day he was going out to his father's farm,
and he came upon the murderer suddenly. The
man could not avoid him; they were alone;
S. John was armed, the other was not. But now
that the moment demanded his act, and when the
other begged to be spared, prayed for mercy and
forgiveness in the name of Christ, S. John could
not kill him. He fled into the neighbouring church
of San Miniato and prostrated himself in floods of
tears before a Crucifix; the Crucifix bowed Its head.
Later, S. John retired to Vallombrosa, where he
founded an Order famous for its austerity.

PLATE XXIV : *from a predella*
by the Blessed Angelico (No. 663)

SAINT JULIAN

The youthful martyr here illustrated has as a distinguishing mark a line of blood round his head; the same figure occurs in a picture by Lorenzo di Credi once at Lockinge*, where he is called S. Julian.

I believe that that name is right. But the S. Julian, Patron of Rimini, proposed for the Credi picture does not suit; he was one of the two S. Julians tied up in a sack full of vipers and thrown into the sea. S. Julian of Emesa would be a little better; he had a nail driven into his head, but it was apparently only one nail, and there should also be marks on his hands. I am fairly confident that S. Julian, husband of S. Basilissa, is the true identification; one of his tortures was that he was scalped.

The disentangling of these and many other S. Julians is an arduous problem; the old painters or their advisers were probably themselves in a muddle. In many cases, including even the present one, the celebrated S. Julian Hospitator may have been intended, with the emblems of some more obscure S. Julian attached to him.

S. Julian Hospitator was hunting a stag; it spoke, and told him he would kill his own parents. S. Julian fled into a far country, where he married. His father and mother set out in search of him and reached his castle when he was away; his wife, learning who they were, put them in her own bed while she went to church. S. Julian returned and found what he thought were his wife and her lover in bed together; he killed them both with his sword.

S. Julian and his wife in their penitence founded a hospital near a dangerous river; and S. Julian ferried travellers across. Long after, in the middle of a freezing night, there came a pitiful call for the ferry; S. Julian brought in a leper half dead from cold, whom he put in his own bed to warm him. Soon the leper became a resplendent figure, which ascended into heaven saying, *Julian, Christ accepts your repentance*. The story has been re-told by Flaubert.

* The illustration on the opposite page is from an altarpiece, other parts of which Credi is known to have repaired; he may have noticed this very figure.

PLATE XXV : *from a predella
by the Blessed Angelico (No. 663)*

SAINT LUCY

S. Lucy is properly shown with a sword in her neck; this is distinctive, but the painters found it awkward. A commoner attribute, therefore, is a lamp, which is perhaps merely a pun on the name.

From the end of the XIV century, I believe, it became more usual to show her with two eyes on a dish.* According to some critics, an eye is a shining thing and is merely an emblem equivalent to the lamp; they say this must be so, since there exist S. Lucies carrying half a dozen or more eyes. This is indeed the case in four XV century Sienese pictures at least, but it is very unusual to find more than two eyes; I cannot help feeling that the rare local traditions of many eyes are due not to a general belief that the eyes are an emblem, but to a few people's personal view that that is so, and their desire to make it quite clear.

According to other critics, S. Lucy has taken over the attribute from another (Saint ?) Lucy, said to have died in 1420 (*sic*). She was pestered by a young man, and when she asked what it was that attracted him, " Your eyes, your eyes " was all he could say. So she cut them out with a penknife and sent them to him on a dish. *Cette action héroïque eut deux excellents résultats :* the young man reformed and died in the odour of sanctity, and Christ gave Lucy a new pair of eyes far more beautiful than before.

* Two eyes on a book is the attribute of S. Ottilia.

PLATE XXVI : *from a picture by Cima in the Gulbenkian Collection*
on loan to the National Gallery

SAINT MARGARET

S. Margaret was imprisoned, and later beheaded, for her faith. In prison, Satan in the form a dragon swallowed her; but she made the sign of the Cross and he burst.

> *Maiden Margrete*
> *Stood still as any stone,*
> *And that loathly worm*
> *To her-ward gan gone,*
> *Took her in his foul mouth*
> *And swallowed her flesh and bone.*
> *Anon he brast—*
> *Damage hath she none!*

The last line is perspicuously illustrated by Margaritone; her martyr's crown is not even awry.

S. Margaret is invoked against the pains of childbirth; it is said that she requested and was granted a helpful power at such times because of her escape from the dragon.

PLATE XXVII: *from a picture by Margaritone (No. 564)*

MARTYRS

The history-book of the Saints is sodden with blood; some painters, especially the Germans, have revelled in it. Yet it is possible to represent Martyrs without being disgusting.

The Virgin Martyrs here reproduced are not all identifiable. The figure on the extreme right is S. Margaret, who by means of a Cross or by making the sign of the Cross escaped from a dragon, as explained on the previous page. The next is, of course, S. Catherine of Alexandria, and the figure on the extreme left S. Agnes with her lamb.

The Virgin crowned with red and white roses is no other than S. Cecilia, who soon after this picture was painted became the Patroness of Music. S. Cecilia and her husband Valerian (they remained chaste) were crowned by an angel with the roses of Paradise, which cannot fade or lose their scent or be seen but by those who love Chastity. A similar figure with the name inscribed exists on another of Angelico's pictures, so the identity here is certain. There exist S. Cecilias with both the crown of roses and an organ or organ pipes by Luini at S. Maurizio, Milan, and by a Follower of Signorelli (Baldinacci ?) at Città di Castello.

PLATE XXVIII: *from a predella by the Blessed Angelico (No. 663)*

SAINT MARY MAGDALENE

PLATE XXIX : *from an altarpiece by Mantegna (No. 274)*

SAINT MATTHEW

The Evangelists when shown together are
distinguished from other Saints in often
appearing not in their bodily form at all,
but only their symbols; the Angel for
S. Matthew, the Lion for S. Mark, the
Ox for S. Luke, the Eagle for S. John.

PLATE XXX : *from a picture by Tura (No. 772)*

SAINT NICHOLAS (1)

Santa Claus is the Patron of children, although he never joined in childish games and on the very day of his birth stood up precociously in his bath; perhaps it is because he restored three children to life, who during a famine had been salted down for food. His most frequent attribute, as here, is three golden balls, which stand probably for the dowries he gave to three poor girls.*

Once a man borrowed money of a Jew, and swore on the altar of S. Nicholas to repay it; he did not, and the Jew brought him before the judge. The borrower had hidden the money in a hollow walking-stick, which he asked the Jew to hold for him. He then stated on oath that he had returned the money, was acquitted, took back his stick from the Jew and walked off; a passing cart ran over him and broke open the stick, so the fraud was revealed. S. Nicholas *might* therefore be the Patron Saint of Lenders, and might have occasioned the three gold balls of the pawnbrokers.

* This is clearly indicated in an Andrea da Salerno at Naples.

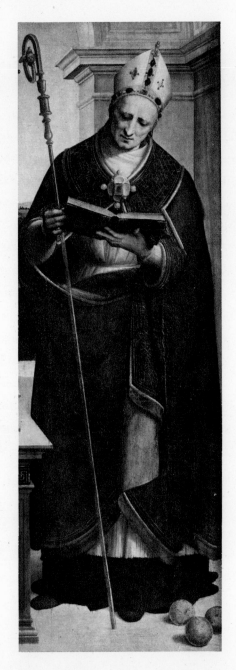

PLATE XXXI: *from an altarpiece by Raphael (No.* 1171)

SAINT NICHOLAS (2)

S. Nicholas took strong measures to suppress the worship of Diana in favour of Christianity. The devil was angry and made an oil that burns stone and is not extinguished by water. Then the devil disguised himself as a pious woman, and said to some pilgrims who were voyaging by sea to visit S. Nicholas, " Give him this oil, and for my sake anoint the walls of his house with it." An image of S. Nicholas at once appeared and told them, " That was the foul Diana ; and to prove I speak true, cast out this oil on the water." The pilgrims did so, and the sea burst into flame.

PLATE XXXII : *from a picture by Margaritone (No. 564)*

SAINT PAUL
THE HERMIT

This S. Paul was the first hermit in the
Egyptian desert. S. Anthony, who with
the aid of two friendly lions buried him,
took away his dress of matted palm leaves
and wore it himself on Feast Days.

PLATE XXXIII : *from a predella by
the Blessed Angelico (No. 663)*

SAINT PHILIP BENIZZI

In the XIII century seven noble Florentine youths banded themselves together in honour of the Virgin. The place of worship they chose was a chapel then outside the walls of Florence; the people seeing them go by so often spoke of them as the Servants of Mary, and thus the Order of the Servi came into being. The chapel is now the church of the Annunziata, famous for its frescoes by Andrea del Sarto and others.

S. Philip Benizzi was not one of the original seven, but is the Saint of the Servite Order. He spent his whole life in doing good, especially in appeasing the political broils that distracted every town of Italy. He had been beatified but not canonized when this picture was painted; possibly the halo has been added.

PLATE XXXIV: *from an altarpiece by Romanino (No. 297)*

SAINT PROCLA

S. Procla or Claudia Procula is supposed to have been the name of Pilate's wife, who thus besought her husband : " Have thou nothing to do with that righteous Man ; for I have suffered many things this day in a dream because of Him."—(*Matthew*, xxvii, 19.)

A more prominent figure in the illustration is, of course, Pontius Pilate himself ; but his status is more dubious. He has indeed also been canonized—by the Abyssinians ; and several writers of the East have taken a very favourable view of him. " All the generations and the families of the Gentiles shall call thee blessed, because in thy days were fulfilled all those things which were spoken by the prophets." It has nevertheless been customary in the West to regard Pilate as a criminal ; and hate has been fruitful of legend. Judas Iscariot, for instance, is said to have killed his father and married his mother, Pilate being largely responsible.

His end was told, subject to variations, as follows. The Emperor Tiberius had been cured of fever and ulcers and nine kinds of leprosy at the mere sight of S. Veronica's Holy Napkin ; he therefore summoned Pilate to Rome for the crime of authorizing the Crucifixion. Tiberius was full of anger against Pilate, but his anger vanished when Pilate was brought before him ; when he was taken away, it raged again ; when he was brought back, it evaporated once more. This was due to Pilate's being clothed in the seamless tunic of Jesus Christ ; as soon as he was stripped of that, Tiberius suffered no abatement of his fury, and Pilate on being condemned to death committed suicide. His body was cast into the Tiber, then into the Rhone at Vienne (apparently confounded with Gehenna !), then buried near Lausanne ; but in each case the water or the land were convulsed in constant disturbance. At last it was thrown into " a deep pit all environed with mountains " ; this is apparently the Lake of Lucerne, beneath a mountain cloud-capped or *pileatus*, whose name could simply be changed into Pilate's own. He is said to rise above the surface of the water every Good Friday, and feebly wash his hands.

PLATE XXXV: *from a picture by the Master of Kappenberg (No.* 2154)

SAINT RAPHAEL

The story of Tobias and the Angel is in the strange *Book of Tobit*. Tobit, who was blind, sent his son Tobias to collect a debt; Tobias set off with his dog and with S. Raphael, who under the name of Azarias agreed to accompany him for a drachm a day. When they reached the Tigris, Tobias went down to wash, and a fish would have devoured him; but the angel told Tobias to take the fish, and they set aside the heart and the liver and the gall, and ate the rest. When they came to Rages, Tobias married his cousin Sara, who had been given to seven men, and they had all died in the marriage chamber; but Tobias took the ashes of perfume and laid on them some of the heart and liver of the fish, and made a smoke with it, which drove the evil spirit out of Sara. The angel meanwhile had obtained the money owing, and they all returned to Tobit; Tobias anointed his father's eyes with the gall of the fish, and his blindness was cured.

In pictures Tobias is shown carrying a small fish, which obviously could not have eaten him and has not been eaten by him. The subject was very popular, probably because Tobias and S. Raphael were types of man and his guardian angel.

PLATE XXXVI: *from a picture by Lorenzo di Credi (No. 593)*

SAINT ROCH

S. Roch was invoked against the Plague. His fame might have been confined to his native Montpellier ; but it is said that the Plague broke out at the Council of Constance, where some delegates had heard of S. Roch, he was invoked and the Plague ceased. The popularity of S. Roch soared ; and then the Venetians stole his relics.

They had long before stolen S. Mark, deceiving the Alexandrian customs officials by an ingenious ruse. They thought they had stolen S. Nicholas ; but the counter-claim of the people of Bari is admitted, not so much because the Bari party carried off S. Nicholas first as that the body at Bari is a constant source of miracles. Criticism has been more generous to the Venetians about S. Roch, despite suspicious circumstances ; for S. Roch's body was legitimately transferred from Montpellier to Arles and remained there, and yet the Venetians claim to have got it from Voghera.

In any case, the S. Roch of Venice was a source of prosperity, which has been reflected in the arts ; Tintoretto especially profited. The plate shows the Church and School of S. Roch at Venice, built upon *stolen* foundations.

PLATE XXXVII : *a picture by Canaletto (No. 937)*

SAINT SEBASTIAN

S. Sebastian, martyr, was pierced with arrows (he was killed later by other means). From very early times he has been invoked against the Plague, perhaps because the onset of the Plague was conceived as a cloud of arrows from an angry Heaven. A greatly increased demand for pictures against the Plague coincided with the time when painters were glad of any excuse for painting the nude ; a naked figure pierced with a varying number of arrows is therefore frequently met with in old pictures. It should, however, be added that S. Sebastians in costume, holding one or more arrows as an emblem, continued to be painted throughout the XV century, especially in the Venetian School.

PLATE XXXVIII: *from a predella by Crivelli (No. 724)*

SAINT SYLVESTER

Angelico in his picture has given S. Sylvester the most prominent possible place; and indeed S. Sylvester was very important. The past tense is necessary; S. Sylvester *was* the man to whom the Donation of Constantine was made, which *was* the legal justification for the temporal power of the Popes. But the Donation of Constantine is a forgery.

Dante in his interview with the simoniac Nicholas III passes from tremendous humour through all the degrees of invective, until with the Donation of Constantine the tone becomes despairing :—

> *Ahi, Costantin, di quanto mal fu matre,*
> *non la tua conversion, ma quella dote*
> *che da te prese il primo ricco patre !**

Dante does not in fact put S. Sylvester in Hell; but he neglects to find him in Paradise either.

---

* O Constantine, alas, what evil has been caused, not by your conversion but by that Gift you gave to the first wealthy Pope.

PLATE XXXIX : *from a predella by
the Blessed Angelico (No. 663)*

SAINT THECLA

The figure illustrated is, from its position on the picture, the first female martyr; that was S. Thecla. Her character was that of perfect disciple. and the man she sat at the feet of was S. Paul. She is invoked in the Catholic prayers for the dying, and is therefore well known; but her appearance in pictures is rare.

It might be thought that she has here no attribute except a martyr's palm; but she has one. S. Paul often made dangerous journeys; S. Thecla asked his leave to accompany him, and offered to cut her hair short and put on male attire. This Shakespearean incident was forbidden by the Apostle; and I have no doubt that that is why Angelico has shown her with long hair.

PLATE XL : *from a predella by the Blessed Angelico (No. 663)*

SAINT THOMAS À BECKET

In the history of the struggles between Church and State, the chapter concerning Becket and Henry II is one of the most interesting ; S. Thomas indeed lost his life, but it was nevertheless a great victory for the Church. The king was forced to do public penance, and Becket was canonized almost at once. The pilgrimage to Canterbury became one of the most important in Europe (being of use, incidentally, to Chaucer) ; and the fame of the English Martyr spread far and wide, as this picture from Fiesole testifies.

The Church's victory did not endure in this country ; when Henry VIII had quarrelled with the Pope, he issued a Proclamation that Becket was not a saint, but a rebel.

Plate XLI : *from a predella by*
the Blessed Angelico (*No. 663*)

SAINT URSULA

The extraordinary story of S. Ursula and the 11,000 Virgins has been the occasion of diverse effects. Carpaccio used it to introduce Venetian costume, Claude here made it an excuse for painting light and air, and it inspired the Blessed Hermann Joseph with the following mystic verses :—

> *O quam estis vos securae !*
> *Deo semper fruiturae,*
> *Cum quo estis permansurae,*
> *Numquam eo carituae,*
> *Quem videtis, quem tenetis,*
> *Qui vos ulnis stringit laetis,*
> *Serena ridens facie.*
>
> *O reginae puellares,*
> *Passione sancta pares,*
> *Deo vos familiares,*
> *Praedilectae, singulares,*
> *Nunc florete, nunc gaudete,*
> *Semper novae, semper laetae,*
> *Festivum chorum ducite.*
>
> *Vos jucundae philomelae,*
> *Quarum turbae sunt undenae,*
> *Sponsae Dei, Deo plenae,*
> *Decantate laudem bene,*
> *Virginales per choreas,*
> *Et coelestes per plateas,*
> *Jucundum carmen dicite.*

PLATE XLII : *a picture by Claude (No.* 30)

SAINT ZENO

S. Zeno of Verona is one of the bishops who carry a fish. He gave two men three fishes and they stole a fourth; but they could not cook it—in boiling water it remained alive! Alternatively, S. Zeno was fond of a day's fishing in the Adige.

These charming legends contrast with the story of S. Ulrich, the fish-bishop of Augsburg. S. Ulrich was supping one Thursday with Bishop Wolfgang; time passed, and they did not notice that it was already Friday. Suddenly a messenger came from the Emperor; he stared and stared at a goose on the table. S. Ulrich (whose motives are variously interpreted) cut off a drumstick and gave it to the messenger. The latter hastened back to the Emperor, and began to explain what he had found S. Ulrich doing on a Fast Day; to illustrate his point, he put his hand in his bag and brought out—a fish!

PLATE XLIII: *from a picture by Montagna (No. 3074)*

SAINT ZENOBIUS

S. Zenobius, Bishop, is one of the Patrons
of Florence ; he appears not infrequently
in Florentine pictures, usually ·without
attribute.

The plate illustrates his first step on
the path to sanctity. S. Zenobius was
brought up as a pagan ; in due course his
parents, who were of good family, arranged
his marriage with a suitable bride. S.
Zenobius positively refused to marry,
walked off and was immediately baptized a
Christian. Botticelli has not neglected
the humour of the scene.